LOVE
AND
OTHER
THINGS

LOVE AND OTHER THINGS

A COLLECTION OF POETRY

MANJOT MANN

LOVE AND OTHER THINGS
A COLLECTION OF POETRY

iUniverse books may be ordered through booksellers or by contacting:

iUniverse
1663 Liberty Drive
Bloomington, IN 47403
www.iuniverse.com
1-800-Authors (1-800-288-4677)

ISBN: 978-1-5320-6750-1 (sc)
ISBN: 978-1-5320-6751-8 (e)

Print information available on the last page.

iUniverse rev. date: 02/11/2019

This book is dedicated to Sophia.

Introduction

No poem is about a single person or a solitary moment in time. They are moments that happened, didn't happen, should have happened, or could have happened.

This collection has been simmering in my journal for years and I feel privileged to be able to share these snippets of love with you.

I hope these poems make you feel.

Yours,

Manjot Mann

Lost Loves

Rosie

I still think of you sometimes
how you said my name with a shy smile
I think of your smell
your small stooped stature
how no matter how sick you were
your hair always looked the same
a thick, vibrant brown against all odds
I think about the end
how your voice changed
strained from never being used
how you sat numb among family
seeing lips move but hearing no sound
you must have missed soft laughter
quiet sighs
I think of you so much
but I try to forget
because all that remains in my mind is the end
the brightly lit hospital
the bed
your nails painted a shocking purple
and how you left with a breath we never saw
just a machine telling us it was over
I'm growing a little girl now
and I can't help but wonder if some part of you
is coming back to us as all

Sister

If I could just catch you
it would be easier
throw you in the back of the car
make you talk
aren't we still family?
and you would reply
of course
shit happens
but we move on

a ludicrous notion
the naivety of a child
the stink of a starving man

once upon a time
a girl wished for laughter unbounded
got the opposite in return
rivers of earthquakes
some call it divorce
I call it a lackadaisical experiment
in shoulda, coulda, woulda

the road in front is empty
sister, where are you?
if I walk on heat soaked cement
head towards you
will you embrace me with open arms?
soak my sweat and callus havocked feet in warm water
wash away the tears?

I imagine your features have sharpened
to those of moms
small right angle nose
mouse like eyes that see everything
possibly missing your other half
I hope

I imagine that someone somewhere
has done an experiment
about indifference, jealousy, rage
how they combine into a ball
and define family
and then shatter the pieces
like a Christmas ornament

if words are painted with hate
they're still words
aren't they?

all roads lead to you
I'm coming home sister
if you'll have me

Why?

They could have been someone
if you had just let them be
but you sunk your teeth in
now they're just a number
a collection of
somebodies

Please stay

She had thought about it before
at night
when he was still alive
his warm body a steady presence
she thought
if he ever goes
I will lose it

and so when they came to the door
the Mounties hat in hand
she decided
to hell with it
he's still alive
and shut the door

she assumed widows quivered
like a flower in the throes of passion
she wouldn't

she headed into her room
changed
went to work
they all looked with pity
of course they will she thought
but she mirrored it back
the woeful expressions
the gentle shaking of the head
the not quite but almost oh…I'm
yea don't care

death is a mindset not a reality

she went home
made dinner
set the table
and waited
he was never late but never on time
he was a presence
laughter filling
all the open spaces
suddenly the world seemed so small
so unprepared
to handle his absence

she cleaned up the dinner plates
lethargy her friend
there is a knock on the door
tentative afraid
oh…I'm…

she goes to bed
on his side not hers
breaking the pattern
but she thinks maybe
it's okay

he'll embrace her insanity
the rough patch of her mind
the inability to wrap her arms around gone

I love you now
I loved you then
I always have
and I always will

Ma

She was someone to me too
I lost her just like you
left with a breath we never saw
a silent sigh
amongst sobs of Ma

Love isn't always him

Baby

I'm not a maybe place for your heart
you either take all of me
or none at all

It was gift-wrapped

You are so much more
than the lies
he passes you

Lost girl

I saw a woman once
she looked like you
painted so many colors
I couldn't tell if she wanted to be seen
or hidden from view

I thought of reaching out
and saying hello
she might have been your reflection
I thought I knew her
you know

but on second glance
I had a change of heart
she was missing something
I couldn't count all the cracks

the fellow beside her
he looked like a gem
reaching out and tugging her along
as if she were an extension of him

on second thought she was nothing like you
she was a waif in the wind
and you would never let that be you

Scream it

Your voice should be bigger than his
shadow
better yet
there should be no shadow

I'm not your life support

I could breathe forgiveness into you
but then you would think
it was yours to take
not mine to give

Almost but not quite

I slipped the other day
I almost told you
how you tore me open in everyway

I've always been whole

A broken me
is nothing compared to a broken you
I don't need to be a we
but you've always needed a me and you

Love is a thing

Johnny

She's the queen
but he's never the king
fell from paradise
with the swig of a bottle

Never enough

It's always an impossible choice
love blurs sense
I love you but I love the rush more

I did it for love

I did it for the boys

It's a bang with a boom
and a boo
with a who?
and I woulda
I shoulda
but I couldn't
and now
there's blood
and a person
and no beat
and it hurts
but I got no place to go, see?
and there's a rancid, decrepit,
smell in the air
so I drop the gun
I run
I'm so out of here
weooooo weooooooo
I'll run fast
I'll run hard
I'll go far, you'll see
I'm just a kid
on the wrong side
you all know
you've met
one,
two, three, four,
five of me

You taught me love

I love you

You taste like my teenage dreams
the ones that said
you were too good for me

you taste like the doubt
the lies I wove and spun
that reminded me
only pretty girls won

it was just a moment
a touch of your hand
we've created so much now
our own little fairytale land

It's that alone
kind of love

Tell me why

It's not the cage that interests me
it's how you got there

I love old me
new me every me

I think I know her

knock knock
just checking to see
if I'm still there
a loose image of me
just bones of a girl
tossed into a woman
now a mother
and still dust inside
bearing one truth and another
building my fortress my wall
to keep you safe inside
this time

Love made me hide

Please

I am unhinged without you
hidden for so long
between dust and words
caressing hands of strangers
I thought I could hide forever
from one page to the next
no one would think to look
behind mounds of paper
other stories
other lives
you're asking me to take a breath now
I'd much rather not

Love notes to myself

You'll find a way out

I need you to hear your own voice
it's a fury
it's a fire
a light

Open wound

I didn't know how deep I could cut
until I opened my mouth
and heard the voice of a stranger
so long had I kept her there
I didn't recognize her
for me

You are enough

I can hear you roar
even if it's only a ripple
in the sea

My love for you

Don't grow up

I breathe in and I hold
just for a moment
I freeze time

It's always been you

I want you to be liquid fire
a breath fleetingly no ones
and yet everywhere at once
leaving unapologetic footprints
as you carve yourself into you

I'm not sure it's worth it

I worry about you
suffocating
under four letters

L-O-V-E

It was just a word
then I met you

Always

I want to wash away the doubt
demand it leave your eyes
uncertainty is a shadow
a coward in disguise

you're loved
you're wanted

that's all you need to know
the rest is dust and darling
I'll blow away every woe

I'll be superwoman

I need to grow
because what I do
becomes your legacy
not mine

Fire

You are my greatest adventure
the moments I didn't know
I needed

Dear Sophia

I hope you find love in all the right places
a city
a book
the sunset
the sea
chocolate melting on your tongue
sand in your feet
the constant in life

You are you

You can be whoever you want
your life is a blank page
begin
and start

Be never ending

Do you see how vast it is
you could disappear
or you could wake up one day
and realize
that it's all yours for the taking

Be everything

I worry about all of my expectations for you
I worry that I wont realize
they're not meant for you

My girl

The love will astound you they said
they were wrong
it's a gravity of it's own
words can't own it

Love all women

Giver

It's a little too much
don't you think
I fight you fight we regress
and the struggle never ends
I am woman and yet
synonymous with so much sadness
when happiness
is born out of me

Printed in the United States
By Bookmasters